HOW THEY LIVED

AN AMERICAN PIONEER FAMILY

ROBIN MAY

Illustrated by
Mark Bergin

Wayland

F

HOW THEY LIVED

An American Pioneer Family
A Crusading Knight
A Family in World War II
An Ice Age Hunter
A Medieval Serf
A Plantation Slave
A Roman Centurion
A Saxon Farmer
A Victorian Factory Worker

First Published in 1985 by
Wayland (Publishers) Limited
49 Lansdowne Place, Hove
East Sussex BN3 1HF, England

© Copyright 1985 Wayland (Publishers) Limited

British Library Cataloguing in Publication Data
May, Robin
An American pioneer family. — (How they lived)
1. Frontier and pioneer life — United States —
History — 19th century
I. Title   II. Bergin, Mark   III. Series
973   F596

ISBN 0 85078 548 0

Typeset by Planagraphic Typesetters Limited
Printed in Italy by G. Canale & C.S.p.A., Turin
Bound in the UK by The Bath Press

CONTENTS

A LONG, HARD JOURNEY   4

THE COVERED WAGON   6

BUILDING A HOME   8

FAMILY LIFE   10

WHAT PIONEERS WORE   12

FOOD AND DRINK   14

HEALTH AND SICKNESS   16

GOING TO SCHOOL   18

FACING DANGERS   20

A TRIP TO TOWN   22

RELIGION   24

RECREATION   26

CRIME AND PUNISHMENT   28

THE END OF THE FRONTIER   30

GLOSSARY   31

MORE BOOKS TO READ   31

INDEX   32

A Long, Hard Journey

They were nearing their journey's end. Everyone was walking beside the covered wagons that were inching their way along a dangerous part of the trail through the Rocky Mountains. There was a gorge on one side and a fast-flowing river far below on the others. A swerve to the right or left would have ended in disaster.

These pioneers, and others like them, made history. They had braved marauding Indians, dust storms, and extremes of heat and cold on their 3,000-kilometre (1,800-mile) crossing of North America, from Independence, in the state of Missouri, to the 'promised land' of Oregon, on the Pacific coast.

As they made their way west, the pioneers crossed an area known as the Great American Desert. It was a vast, treeless region with hard-packed soil

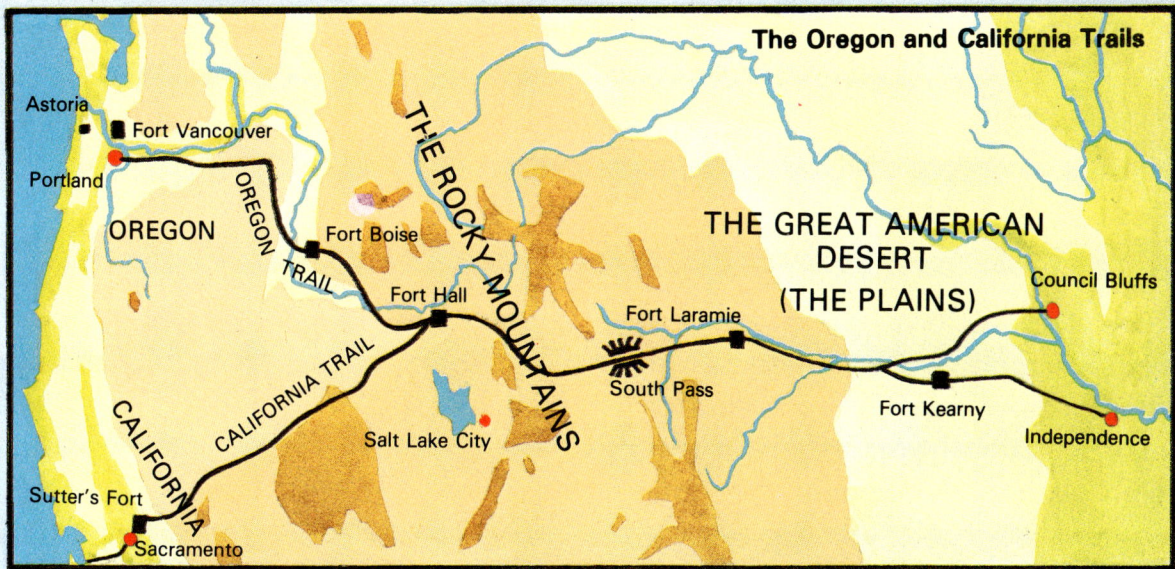

The map shows The Oregon and California Trails with the following labels: Astoria, Fort Vancouver, Portland, OREGON, OREGON TRAIL, Fort Boise, Fort Hall, THE ROCKY MOUNTAINS, South Pass, Fort Laramie, THE GREAT AMERICAN DESERT (THE PLAINS), Council Bluffs, Fort Kearny, Independence, CALIFORNIA TRAIL, CALIFORNIA, Salt Lake City, Sutter's Fort, Sacramento.

The route to the West took the brave pioneers across the Great American Desert and over the Rocky Mountains.

which was thought infertile. It stretched from the Missouri River to the Rocky Mountains and from Texas to the Canadian border. In the 1860s and after, however, a new wave of pioneers swarmed on to this land, renamed the plains, which was found very suitable for farming. This book will tell you about the people who made the new lands their home.

THE COVERED WAGON

There was nothing grand about a covered wagon. It was usually a converted farm wagon. There were some wagons, called prairie schooners, which were purpose-built for long journeys. Most of these big wagons were used for trading.

The covered wagon was home for the pioneers on their long trip west. They packed as much as they could into them — tools for farming and building, cooking utensils, bedding, weapons, food, water and a few luxuries like furniture. Some things were tied to the sides of the wagon. Wagons were usually pulled by oxen. As the journey progressed the animals grew weak. Many things had to be discarded to lighten their load.

Wagon trains were often led across the plains by a guide.

A pioneer family and their covered wagon 'home'.

Inside the covered wagon was a bed like a wooden box. It was four metres (thirteen feet) long and about a metre (three feet) wide. The whole family slept here. Usually the wagon's canvas cover was kept up as protection against dust and rain, but in very hot weather it was folded back.

Wagons had no springs. They often lost a wheel or broke apart and many families never finished the journey.

On the trails to Oregon and California it was vital for pioneers to get to their destination before the winter snows blocked the mountain passes.

When the long journey came to an end each family settled on a chosen spot. Wagons that had survived were again used for farm work.

Sometimes the wagon trains were attacked by bands of Indians.

BUILDING A HOME

In the northwest, with its great forests, homes were built of wood. But on the plains to the east and south there were hardly any trees at all. So the first homes that many pioneers built on the plains were made by digging into a mound or hill. This formed a single cave-like room called a dugout. Dugouts were dirty and unhealthy and were only temporary homes.

Next came a sod-house. Pioneers who built with sod — the earth — became known as sodbusters. The sodbusting age can be said to date from 1862 when the government gave 160 acres (64.8 hectares) to anyone who wanted them for a small fee.

To build a sod-house the sod was cut into blocks three feet (one metre) long. These blocks were used in much the same was as we use bricks today. Spaces were left for windows and a door. Rafters, to support the roof, were made of brushwood. Only families with money could afford a proper timber-framed roof. The roof was made of a layer of prairie grass covered with sods. The spaces between the sods were filled with soil. Doors and windows were covered with buffalo skins or blankets to keep out draughts. A length of pipe through the roof served as a chimney.

Sod-houses were not much healthier than dugouts. It was difficult to keep them dry inside in heavy rain but at least they were cool during the hot summers and warm in the freezing winters. Because the walls were made of earth, sod-houses were also safe from fire.

Sod-houses were built from blocks of earth cut out of the ground.

Early pioneers on the plains made their homes in dugouts (**above left**). *In the northwest, log cabins were more common* (**above right**).

FAMILY LIFE

A pioneer family needed strength and courage to survive. Pioneers had to grow their own food. Corn, or maize, was the main crop. There were no machines to help them farm, and the ground was very hard. Some pioneers had to use axes to break the soil. Oxen or horses were used for jobs like ploughing. All the family helped: the men doing the ploughing and other heavy work; the wives tending a vegetable garden; and the children milking the cows, feeding the animals and collecting chickens' eggs.

Pioneer families were often lonely. The nearest neighbour might be fifty kilometres (thirty miles) away. Many things had to be faced alone. One wife recalled fighting bedbugs and flies all summer and scrubbing floors to keep her house clean. Water had to be pumped out of the well by hand.

Many wives died young and many children died too. Despite this, families were usually large.

On the plains, buffalo droppings were collected for burning on fires.

A large pioneer family seated in front of their sod-house.

A pioneer's wife rarely had time to leave the farm, there was always work to be done. She had to make all the family's clothes, cook the meals, clean the house, bake bread and grow vegetables as well as helping on the farm. Her husband occasionally went into town or visited another farm. A trip to the nearest town was usually made to buy supplies like salt, coffee, flour and seeds for next year's crops. For the pioneer family, life was mostly work and very little play.

WHAT PIONEERS WORE

From the picture on this page you can see the sort of clothes a pioneer family wore. They brought their eastern clothes with them when they came West, but these soon wore out. Then the women had to make new clothes for their families.

Men wore trousers of denim or duck. Both these fabrics are made from cotton and are very hard wearing. Washing and the hot sun soon faded coloured garments. Clothes looked even more faded when a bright, new patch was sewn on to

Pioneers' clothes were usually home made and heavily patched. Women and children often went barefoot.

them. In the winter, some pioneers dressed like trappers in animal skins. Clothes were worn until they could no longer be patched or mended. Men usually had just one pair of trousers. If they needed repairing, the husband went to bed while his wife got out her sewing basket.

Women wore long dresses made from calico, another type of cotton.

Pioneer women wore long dresses made from calico.

Some wore bonnets or shawls around their heads to shade their faces from the burning sun. In towns, pioneers could keep up with fashion. They were helped by a publication called *Godey's Lady's Book.* A poor pioneer wife who liked the look of a silk dress could copy it in cotton.

Shoes were a problem. Many pioneers copied the Indians and wore soft leather moccasins. Boots they bought too big because the leather shrank when it got wet. Most people went barefoot in the summer; women and children usually wore no shoes indoors. In winter, pioneers wrapped rags around their feet because they had no socks.

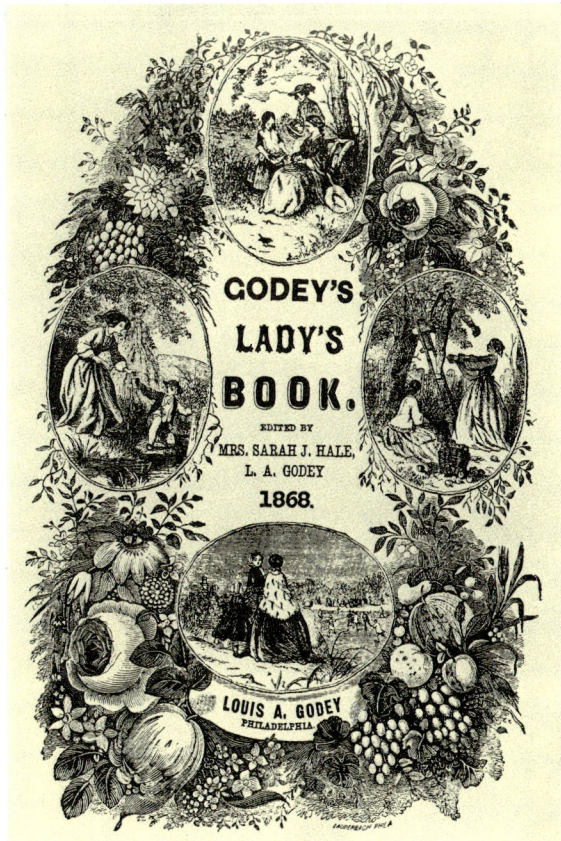

GODEY'S LADY'S BOOK.

EDITED BY
MRS. SARAH J. HALE,
L. A. GODEY
1868.

LOUIS A. GODEY
PHILADELPHIA

Godey's Lady's Book helped pioneer women keep up with the fashions.

FOOD AND DRINK

The first pioneer families in the West enjoyed an excellent diet. They could hunt buffalo, deer, turkey, duck and other wild animals. But by the 1870s much of the wildlife had vanished. The more pioneers there were in the West, the more animals were killed to feed them.

The buffalo was almost wiped out because is provided food, leather, and warm coats. Pioneers suffered by its disappearance but not as much as some Indian tribes who depended on the buffalo completely for food, shelter and clothing.

There were still many small animals and birds to be hunted, but gradually the pioneers had to depend more and more on the crops they could grow and the animals they could raise, like pigs and cows.

There were wild fruits and nuts to be gathered. These were usually preserved for the long winter. Sugar was in very short supply but, in the forested areas, a sweet syrup could be extracted from maple trees.

Corn bread was the main type of bread. It was nourishing but tasteless. Children took sandwiches of corn bread and molasses to school. Some families had to eat lard instead of butter, and turnips instead of potatoes.

There were usually two main meals taken each day and they were rather boring. Here is a typical pioneer family's food for one day:

Breakfast: Corn bread, salt pork and black coffee.
Dinner: Wild greens, boiled pork and cold corn bread washed down with a 'beverage' made from vinegar and brown sugar and warm creek water.

The pioneers' main drink was coffee. During and after the Civil War (1861 to 1865) it was very expensive so coffee was sometimes made with two parts peas to one of coffee.

Hunting by the early pioneers almost wiped out the buffalo.

15

HEALTH AND SICKNESS

In the early 1800s, when pioneers were first settling in the West, there were no hospitals and very few nurses. The nearest doctor was often more than fifty kilometres (thirty miles) away. Doctor's bills were expensive for poor pioneers, but sometimes they could pay him with a horse or a cow. Usually, though, it fell to the neighbours to help the sick and peo-ple gradually learned which herbs and home-made concoctions could be used to cure illness. They made up all kinds of remedies: coal oil for dandruff; sassafras tea to cure spring fever; well-roasted mouse for measles; and nine shotgun pellets swallowed for boils.

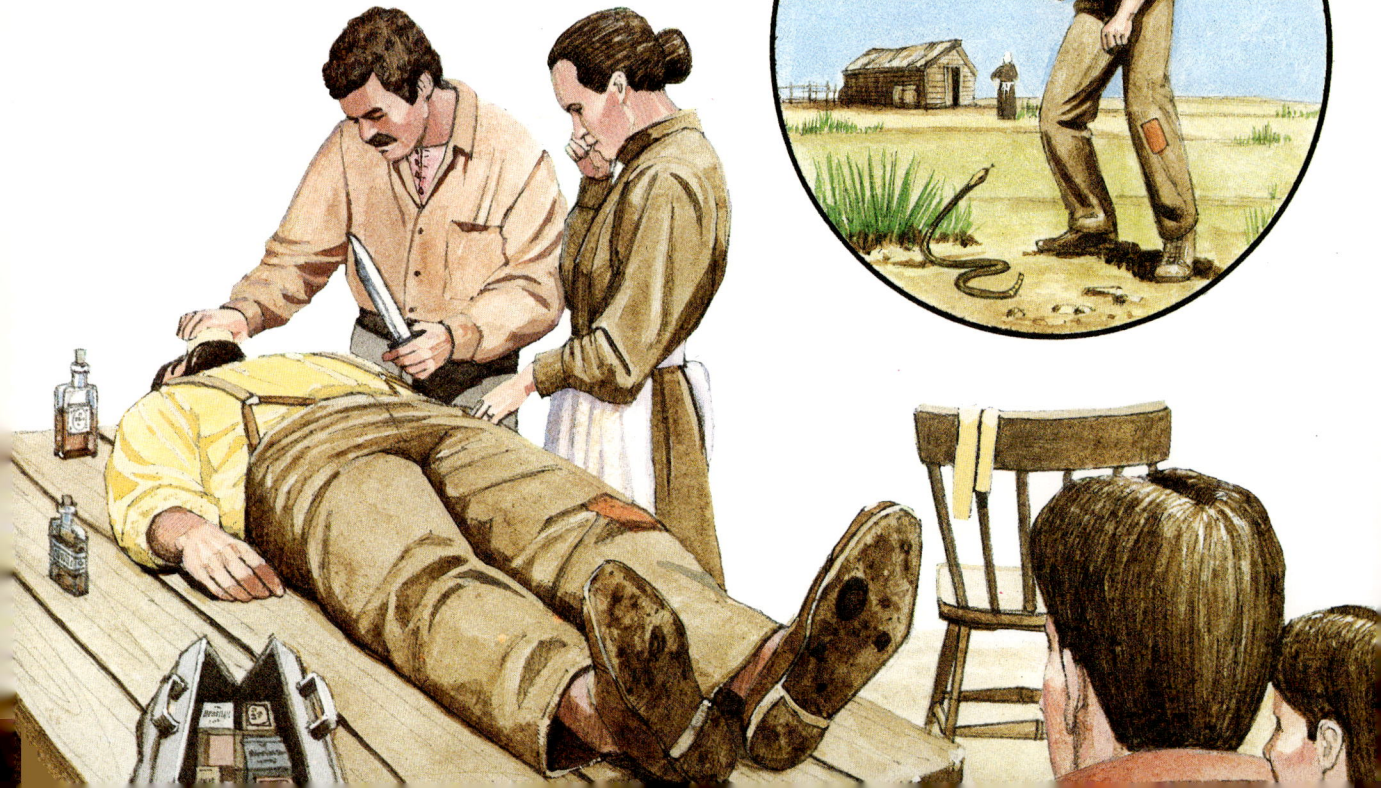

For the pioneers, medical treatment was usually primitive and painful.

Snakes were a hazard. One treatment for a snakebite was to pour turpentine over the bite and make the victim drink whisky. This would at least cheer him up and, so it was thought, counter the effect of the bite.

If surgery was necessary, chloroform was used to put the patient to sleep. It was left to a friend or a member of the patient's family to keep him asleep with more chloroform as the doctor operated.

There were outbreaks of killer diseases in the West like cholera, typhoid, diphtheria and smallpox.

Cholera spread especially quickly and could kill whole families. Dirty water and poor living conditions often encouraged these diseases.

Gunshot wounds, some accidental and some not, were quite common and medical treatment was usually needed. Many babies were born without the help of a doctor. Neighbouring wives gave assistance when they could.

'Quack' doctors, with 'miracle cures' for just about everything, often visited towns in the West.

GOING TO SCHOOL

School teachers were famous and very important figures in the West. They were often only a year or two older than their pupils. Teachers usually worked on their own with no one else to help them. It was not easy.

In the early days teachers often had no house and had to stay with the pupils' families. They went from house to house in turn. When a school was built in the West it was an important event. Parents often paid for the actual building of the school. There were always some people, however, who objected to money being spent on education.

Subjects taught at these schools included history, religion, arithmetic, geography, spelling, agriculture, grammar and reading. Between classes there were playground games.

The opening of a new school was always a great occasion.

Ones that needed no equipment, like hide-and-seek, were especially popular. There were always shortages in the classroom. Some schools opened with no books or desks and not even a blackboard.

Pupils who lived on farms outside the town had to travel a long way to get to school. Children in the West were used to hardships and the walk to school was probably quite enjoyable for them.

On the last day of term there was often an entertainment for the parents. This was an opportunity for them to see what their children had learned. It might include poetry reading, spelling competitions and a picnic. Prizes were given to children who had worked very hard.

Right *A western schoolteacher listens while some of her class read.*

Below *Children of all ages were taught by one teacher.*

FACING DANGERS

Pioneers were constantly aware of the threat of danger. Most feared were the Indians. Before the pioneers came west the land was inhabited by Indians. Gradually the white men settled and farmed on Indian land. The result was racial hatred with victory in the end for the far more numerous white settlers.

Too often badly treated, with promises made by the white man broken, the Indians fought back. Many innocent pioneers lost their lives for the wrongs of others. Today we rightly see the Indian point of view, but we must

A pioneer father returns to find his home destroyed by Indians.

During a range war, pioneers were sometimes killed by wealthy ranchers hungry for their land.

also understand the feelings of a pioneer father returning home to find his family killed and his farm burned to the ground. It was not until the 1890s that the Indian Wars were finally over.

Pioneers had plenty of white enemies too. Ranchers often wanted their land to raise cattle. They sometimes ordered their cowboys to harass sodbusters, even kill them. Women, however, were respected and rarely harmed.

Sometimes full-scale range wars broke out. In 1892, Johnson County, Wyoming, was invaded by 50 Texas gunfighters. They had been hired by local cattle barons to wipe out some of the small ranchers and pioneers in that area. The cattle barons accused them of being rustlers — cattle thieves. The plan didn't work and the gunmen were defeated. After that, settlers and ranchers gradually learned to live together and share the land. Even so they still had natural hazards to face, like killer diseases, dust storms, fires and plagues of locusts.

21

A TRIP TO TOWN

A trip to the nearest town provided the lonely pioneers with a chance to stock up with provisions and to meet their friends.

Going to town in the West could sometimes mean a trip to a place with several thousand inhabitants. More often it meant a long journey to a handful of wooden shacks set in the middle of a wilderness. Yet what we would call a small village was like an oasis in a desert to a lonely pioneer. In town, there would be a chance to do some shopping and to meet people.

Some towns were very tough indeed with cowboys relaxing after a long cattle drive. They were likely to get drunk and start gunfights unless there were brave lawmen to stop them. It was dangerous for pioneers to be in town at the same time as these trouble-makers.

A hardware store and townspeople of Dodge City, Kansas.

The 'Golden Eagle Clothing House' in Wichita, Kansas, in 1878.

Many towns were founded by gold miners or railroad builders. After a period of wildness they settled down. Churches and schools were built. Touring companies brought plays, musical shows and circuses to towns. These were enjoyed by pioneers as well as by townspeople.

Many towns had saloons, although in some areas drinking was forbidden. Gambling was popular in saloons. The average pioneer, however, had very little money to waste on card games and roulette. What he had he needed for equipment and supplies.

23

RELIGION

When the West was first settled there were no churches. Pioneers worshipped at home. Sometimes neighbours took it in turns to hold religious services. A stable, a barn or even the shade of a leafy tree were used as places of worship. Once a town began to take shape, however, plans were soon made for a church to be built.

Some pioneer families took religion very seriously but others were not interested at all. Perhaps they felt they had more important things to do. To remedy this, travelling preachers visited the pioneers, often covering huge distances on horseback or in a wagon. They were nearly always made welcome by the isolated pioneers. The preacher would often stay overnight, and help the family with their chores. Sometimes other families would hear of his arrival and come to hear him preach.

One of the most religious groups of settlers in the West were the Mormons. They were a Christian sect founded in New York State by Joseph Smith in 1830. He and his followers had to move westward because their beliefs made them unpopular. Smith was killed in 1843, but another leader, Brigham Young, took over and led them to Utah's Great Salt Lake. Here they built Salt Lake City. People came from other parts of America, Britain and Europe to join the Mormons.

Opposite *This pioneer church in Moro, Oregon, is still standing.*

Below *Visiting preachers sometimes called on the lonely pioneers.*

Above *A Mormon wagon train heading for Salt Lake City.*

RECREATION

Pioneers were usually so busy working that recreation was a luxury for them. But they did occasionally find time to stop work and enjoy themselves. The most popular sport was racing — on horseback, on foot and, by the 1880s, on bicycle. Many towns soon had their own race tracks, and pioneers would come from miles around to see the races. When they could afford it pioneers enjoyed gambling. If money was short they could bet their clothes.

Baseball and croquet were popular with westerners. Indoor entertainments included card games, like poker, dominoes and reading. Saloons were gambling and drinking centres. There were also billiard saloons and bowling alleys.

All westerners loved to dance though sometimes, especially on ranches, there was a shortage of girls. The problem was solved by some men having to take the female part. There was also a shortage of musicians. Anyone who could play the fiddle could make a lot of money.

Weddings were a good excuse for everyone to have a good time but the most important regular celebration was 4th July, America's Independence Day. This was a big occasion with pioneers coming from far and wide to eat, drink, dance, meet old friends and make new ones. At some stage in the festivities the Declaration of Independence might be read. This dates back to 1776 and marks the breakaway of the American colonies from Britain. At the end of the celebration, the pioneers would drift home saying goodbye to friends they might not see for another year.

A wedding photograph of two Kansas pioneers.

Opposite *4th July, America's Independence Day, was always a cause for celebration.*

CRIME AND PUNISHMENT

Most western crime was committed by gangs of robbers and individual badmen. Pioneers were more concerned with trying to survive and make a living. However, some pioneers and cowboys took to crime as an easier and more exciting way of making a living. The West was so vast that criminals were able to hide out. Most, though, were finally either shot, hanged or imprisoned.

Pioneers were quite prepared to challenge badmen. A classic example

Pioneers sometimes took to crime as a way of making easy money, but they were nearly always caught.

happened at Northfield, Minnesota in 1876. The James-Younger gang of train and bank robbers, led by Jesse James, tried to rob the town's First National Bank. The local citizens got together to protect their money and almost destroyed the gang with a hail of bullets.

Lawmen raised a posse, a group of citizens, to track down criminals. There were also vigilantes, men who took the law into their own hands. They often hung their victims without a proper trial. The crime most usually dealt with by vigilantes was horse-stealing. There were prisons and courts in the West but this form of instant justice too often took the place of a trial before a judge and jury. By 1900 the West was a more settled and civilized place. Crime had become more widespread in the cities.

A group of vigilantes, men who took the law into their own hands.

THE END OF THE FRONTIER

In 1868 America was spanned by rail when lines heading east and west were joined at Promontory Point, Utah. This link, and later lines, made it possible for new settlers to be brought west far more quickly. In 1892 the United States Government announced that no more fertile land was available for settlers.

By the end of the century pioneers and ranchers had settled most of their differences. Towns grew and more were built. Sodbusters were healthier as more doctors came West. Windmills were built to pump water from wells and new machinery and steel ploughs made farming easier. The West had been tamed but older pioneers did not forget the days when they had endured great hardships. They were the true makers of the American West.

By the turn of this century, the West had been tamed. This is the town of Pueblo, Colorado in 1910.

GLOSSARY

American Civil War Conflict which broke out between the northern and southern states of America in 1861 because the people of the south wanted to run their own affairs, which included the right to own slaves. The north won in 1865.

Bedbugs Small blood-sucking insects.

Cattle baron A wealthy rancher.

Indians The natives of America.

Molasses A syrup produced when making sugar. Also known as treacle.

'Quack' doctor A person who knows little about medicine but sells 'miracle cures'.

Roulette A gambling game in which a small ball is dropped on to a revolving wheel with numbered slots in it. People gamble on which slot the ball will end up in.

Saloon A public house or bar.

Sassafras tea A beverage made from the dried root bark of the sassafras tree.

Sect A religious group.

Trapper Someone who catches and kills animals for their skins.

MORE BOOKS TO READ

Non-fiction

Everett Dick, *The Sod-House Frontier 1854-1890*, (University of Nebraska Press 1979)

Pat Hodgson, *Overland to the West*, (Wayland 1978)

Huston Horn, *The Pioneers*, (The Old West series, Time-Life Books 1974)

Robin May, *The American West*, (Macmillan Children's Books 1982)

Robin May, *Daniel Boone and the American West* (Wayland 1985)

Joan Swallow Reiter, *The Women*, (The Old West series, Time-Life Books 1978)

Fiction

Laura Ingalls Wilden, *Little House on the Prairie* (Puffin)

Jack Shaefer, *Shane* (Puffin)

INDEX

Baseball 27
Buffalo 10, 15

California Trail 5, 7
Children 10, 12, 13, 17, 19
Civil War (American) 15,
  31
Clothes 12-13
Cowboys 23
Crime and punishment
  28-29
Crops 10
Croquet 27

Dancing 27
Dangers 17, 20-21
Disease 17, 21
Doctors 16-17
Dugouts 8, 9

Entertainment 23, 27

Family life 10-11
Farming 10, 21
Food and drink 15

Gambling 23, 27
Godey's Lady's Book 13
Gold miners 23
Great American Desert 4, 5
Gunfights 23

Health and sickness 16-17
Homes 8-9
Horse racing 27
Hunting 15

Independence Day 26, 27
Independence, Missouri 4,
  5
Indians 4, 7, 13, 15, 20, 31

James, Jesse 29
Justice 29

Law and order 23, 28-29
Locusts 21
Log cabins 6, 7

Mormons 25

Oregon 4
Oregon Trail 5, 7

Prairie schooners 6
Preachers 24-25

Railroads 23, 30
Range wars 21
Recreation *see*
  Entertainment
Religion 23, 24-25

Saloons 23, 27
Salt Lake City 25
Schools 18-19
Smith, Joseph 25
Snakes 16-17
Sodbusters 8, 9

Towns 11, 22, 23

Vigilantes 29

Wagons 4, 6-7, 25
Weddings 27
Women 10-11, 13

Picture acknowledgements
The pictures in this book were supplied by the following: BBC Hulton Picture Library (The Bettmann Archive Inc.) 9 (right), 13 (bottom), 24, 30; The Kansas State Historical Society (Robin May Collection) 23 (both); The Nebraska State Historical Society (Robin May Collection) 11; The Office of the Secretary of the Interior (Robin May Collection) 19 (bottom); Robin May Collection 29; Peter Newark's Western Americana 6 (top), 7, 9 (left), 15, 19 (top), 27; U.S. Signal Corps (Robin May Collection) 11 (top); U.S. War Department General Staff (Robin May Collection) 26; Work Projects Administration (Robin May Collection) 6 (bottom).

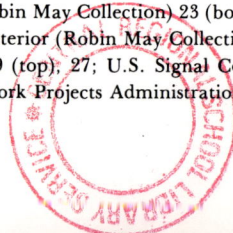